AF251947

Kevin

DURANT

Pete DiPrimio

PURPLE TOAD
PUBLISHING

P.O. Box 631
Kennett Square, Pennsylvania 19348
www.purpletoadpublishing.com

Printing   1   2   3   4   5   6   7   8   9

A Beacon Biography

Big Time Rush
Carly Rae Jepsen
Drake
Harry Styles of One Direction
Jennifer Lawrence
Kevin Durant
Robert Griffin III (RG3)

Publisher's Cataloging-in-Publication Data
DiPrimio, Pete
   Kevin Durant / Pete DiPrimio
     p. cm. – (A beacon biography)
           Includes bibliographic references and index.
           ISBN: 978-1-62469-023-5 (library bound)
           1. Durant, Kevin, 1988– —Juvenile literature. 2. Basketball players – United States – Biography—Juvenile literature.   I. Title.
           GV884.D868 2013
           796.323092—dc23
                                                                                                    2013934694

eBook ISBN: 9781624690266

ABOUT THE AUTHOR: Pete DiPrimio is an award-winning Indiana sports writer, a veteran children's author, and long-time freelance writer. He's also a journalism adjunct lecturer and fitness instructor.

Printed by Lake Book Manufacturing, Chicago, IL

CONTENTS

Kevin Durant played in a college flag football game to relieve his boredom from the NBA strike.

A Kid at Heart

Kevin Durant couldn't take it anymore. The NBA lockout was torture. He couldn't play basketball or work with his Oklahoma City Thunder coaches. NBA officials wouldn't even let him work out at his team's facilities. All because players and owners could not agree on how many millions of dollars each side would make.

Durant, one of the NBA's best players, a 6-foot-9-inch scoring machine, needed action. What could he do on a late October night in 2011?

He tweeted, of course. What would you expect from a guy *Sports Illustrated* ranks among the nation's top 100 Twitter users?

"This lockout is really boring," he tweeted. "Anybody playing flag football in OKC?"

"OKC" is short for Oklahoma City. In nearby Stillwater, Oklahoma State student George Overbey read Durant's tweet and invited him to play for his Sigma Nu fraternity team in an intramural flag football game—basically a pickup game—at the university.

In normal times, Oklahoma City team officials, who pay Durant $13.6 million a year, would make him stay far away from anything like this to avoid the risk of injury. But because of the lockout, Durant was free to do what he wanted. What this 23-year-old wanted to do was to have fun. He told Overbey he would play.

When Durant drove to Oklahoma State, he found that about 500 people had showed up to watch him play. A two-time NBA scoring champ, he played quarterback and defensive back in the flag football game. He threw four touchdowns and intercepted two passes. He was all over the field. Everybody had fun—even the opposing players.

Sigma Nu won, but then had to forfeit for using a player who was not in the fraternity. Nobody cared—certainly not Durant, who enjoyed the moment.

He had lots of moments to enjoy during the lockout, which lasted from July to December of 2011. Durant played in pickup basketball games, summer leagues, and events all over the world, from New York City to Washington D.C., Los Angeles to Baltimore, and the Philippines to China.

This wasn't surprising. While some NBA players took it easy during the lockout, Durant worked harder than ever with Justin Zormelo, his personal trainer. They'd start at six in the morning and sometimes wouldn't finish until the evening.

Durant worked hard to maximize

Everybody enjoyed Durant's 66-point pickup game at the Rucker Park basketball court in Harlem, New York, during the 2011 NBA strike.

Durant used part of his free time during the NBA strike to visit China as part of his Far East tour.

his already amazing physical skills. His physique includes a wingspan of 7.5 feet. That means his arms are so long that, stretched out to each side, he has the reach of a 7-foot-6-inch player.

A lot of people have talent, but not everybody wants to work hard enough to take advantage of it. Durant never stops working or learning because he wants to be the world's best player and win championships. He said his 2012 Olympic experience really helped him as a player and as a team leader.

"I learned how to be a better leader and hopefully I'll bring it back to Oklahoma City and become a better player," he told NBA.com. "I know I have a long way to go. I just have to keep improving."

MONTROSE
3
CHRISTIAN

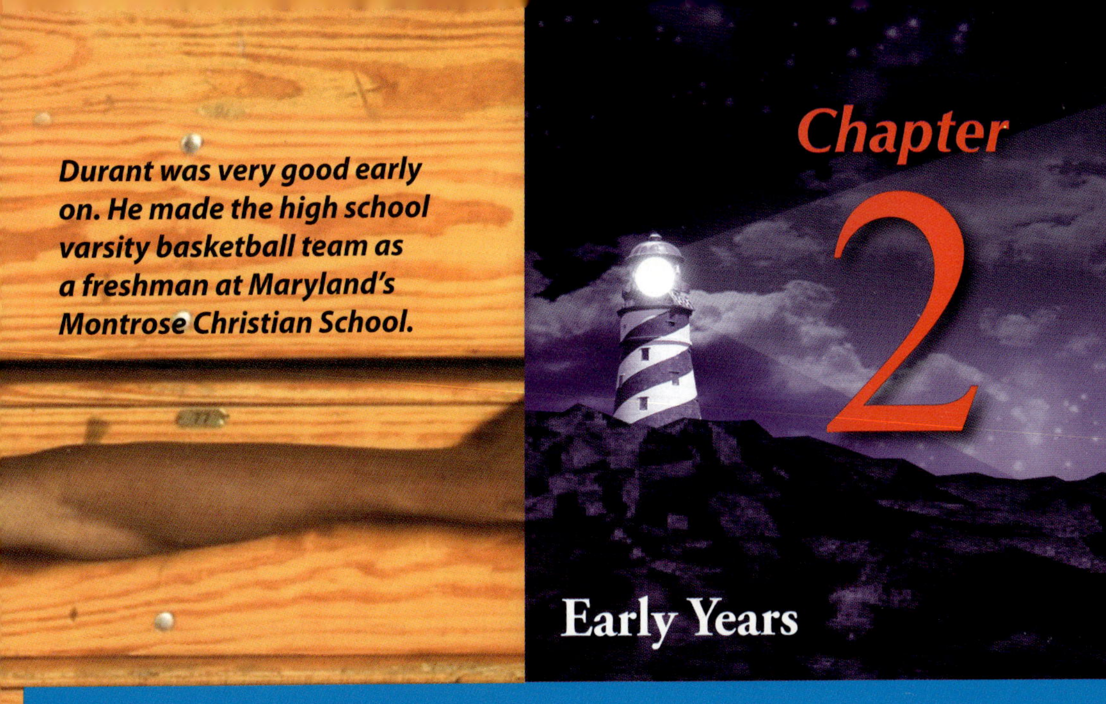

Chapter 2

Early Years

Kevin Wayne Durant was born on September 29, 1988, in Washington, D.C. His parents, Wanda and Wayne Pratt, were hard workers. Wanda worked the night shift for the U.S. Postal Service, loading heavy bags of mail into delivery trucks. Wayne worked for the Library of Congress.

Wanda and Wayne married, but they didn't stay together long. Wayne left a few months after Durant's birth, so he was raised by Wanda and by his grandmother, Barbara Davis. Their family included his sister, Brianna, and two brothers, Tony and Rayvonne.

Durant was always tall and skinny. When he was very young, this was sometimes a problem. Kids at school teased him about his size. He was shy and didn't like to stand out. His mother tried to help by asking his teachers to put him at the ends of lines so others would stand out more, but that only worked for a while. His grandmother kept telling him his height would pay off one day, but he wasn't so sure.

Eventually, Durant began playing sports and his height became an asset, especially when he started playing basketball. He was a big fan of basketball superstar Michael Jordan, who ended his career playing for the NBA's Washington Wizards. Durant finally met Jordan after winning an MVP award at a high school tournament named for Jordan. Still, Kevin's favorite NBA player growing up was the Dallas Mavericks' Vince Carter.

A local Boys and Girls Club where Durant and his brother would go after school also played a big role in Durant's life. They played a lot of different sports there, but basketball was number one.

"I was always in the gym," he said. "People looked at me like I was crazy because I spent so much time there."

Durant quickly became one of the best players around. He joined a travel team with the Amateur Athletic Union (AAU), called the P.G. Jaguars. He and the Jaguars won two national titles, the first when he was 11. He scored 18 points in the second half of that first national title game and was so excited afterward that he began talking about playing in the NBA someday. One of his teammates was Michael Beasley, who would also go on to play in the NBA and remains one of Durant's best friends. Another teammate was Chris Braswell, who would be drafted by the Charlotte Bobcats.

Durant kept improving. He continued to grow taller (he was over six feet tall when he was in middle school) and had a lot of talent. He also worked hard, something he picked up from his mother. She often worked long hours to make sure she had enough money to feed her family.

One of Durant's coaches, Taras "Stink" Brown, was very close to him. Brown had a plan to make him one of the best

A young Kevin Durant

players in the country. Durant was not allowed to play pickup games because those would teach him lazy habits. He could either play in organized games or practice his dribbling and shooting. Sometimes in the summer he worked out as much as eight hours a day.

Brown wanted to make sure Durant never forgot the importance of hard work. Brown constantly told him, "Hard work beats talent when talent fails to work hard."

Durant made varsity as a 6-foot-3 freshman at Montrose Christian School in Rockville, Maryland. He was very good, and some of his older teammates didn't like it. They talked about not passing him the ball and, for a while, he wanted to quit. But he stayed with it. He grew five more inches by the next year. He had guard skills, quickness, and a forward's height. He was almost impossible to stop.

As a junior, he transferred to one of the best basketball schools in the country, Oak Hill Academy in Virginia. He averaged 19.6 points and 8.8 rebounds per game. As a senior, Durant returned to Montrose. There, he averaged 23.6 points, 10.2 rebounds, 3.0 assists, 3.0 steals, and 2.6 blocks while leading Montrose to a 20–2 record and a no. 9 ranking in the final *USA Today* poll.

Durant was ranked as the no. 2 high school player in the country. Every big-time college in the country wanted him. His friend Tywon Lawson, who went on to play for the Denver Nuggets, asked Durant to join him at North Carolina. But University of Texas assistant coach, Russell Springmann, had been recruiting Kevin since he was a high school freshman. A former Texas player, Maurice Evans, was playing for the NBA's Los Angeles Lakers. He sometimes trained with Durant and was very positive about Texas.

Finally, Durant made up his mind. He would be a Texas Longhorn.

A star for Texas, but just for one year.

One and Done

Texas had become a national power under coach Rick Barnes, because of his outstanding recruiting. Durant was the best player in one of the top recruiting classes in the country in 2006. Three other Texas freshmen were nationally ranked among the top 100 newcomers.

Durant weighed only 204 pounds, which is small for someone his height. He arrived in Texas the summer before his freshman year and lifted weights hard. He gained about ten pounds and a lot of strength.

He was one of four freshman starters. The Texas team was very young, but very talented.

Durant could do it all—score, rebound, pass, and block shots. Nobody could stop him. Against Texas Tech, he had 37 points and a career-high 23 rebounds. In the Big 12 Tournament title game against Kansas, he had 37 points, 10.0 rebounds, a career-high
6.0 blocks, and a career-best 6.0 assists (although Texas lost 88–84 in overtime). Durant scored a tournament record 92 points in three games and was named the Most Valuable Player.

Durant and his mother, Wanda Pratt, had a good relationship with Texas coach Rick Barnes.

Durant was so good and so giving and so in tune with his teammates that Coach Barnes rarely needed to call a play. He called Durant a "once-in-a-lifetime guy."

Durant had 30 games of at least 20 points, 11 games of at least 30 points, and his total 903 points were a school and Big 12 single-season record. This ranked as the second most ever scored by a college freshman. Durant's 390 rebounds were the third most by a freshman in NCAA history. He had 20 double-doubles (getting at least 10 points and 10 rebounds in the same game). He led the Big 12, and was ranked fourth nationally, by averaging 25.8 points per game. He averaged 11.1 rebounds and 1.9 blocks. Durant set Big 12 records for scoring (28.9) and rebounding (12.5) in conference games only.

With Durant leading the way, Texas went 25–10 with a top-20 national ranking. The team made the NCAA Tournament as the no. 4 seed. The Longhorns beat New Mexico State in their first game, then lost 87–68 to the University of Southern California in their second game.

Meanwhile, Durant won a slew of national Player of the Year awards, including the John R. Wooden Award. No other freshman had ever done that. He also became just the third freshman to make first-team All-America, joining Wayman Tisdale (1983) and Chris Jackson (1989).

Durant had a decision to make. He could return to school and try to help Texas win a national championship, or he could leave early and enter the NBA Draft.

He chose to leave early. So did Ohio State center Greg Oden. Because both were dominant big men, there was a lot of talk about who should be the no. 1 pick.

Finally, the Portland Trailblazers took Oden as the no. 1 pick for 2007. The Seattle SuperSonics picked Durant at no. 2.

There was a lot of pressure on Durant, but he was more than ready.

Durant's decision to leave college after his freshman year paid off when the Seattle Supersonics made him the no. 2 pick in the NBA draft, the highest ever for a Texas player.

The Pro Challenge

Did Durant have first-game jitters in Denver? No way. He'd played in too many big events for too long to let his first official NBA game rattle him. "I was nervous," he said, "but the butterflies went away." He scored 18 points in that first pro game, which was on Halloween of 2007, and it only got better.

He quickly got used to NBA demands, which included playing a lot more games (82 during the regular season compared to around 30 for college), constant travel (from Boston to Los Angeles and from Minnesota to Miami), and stiff competition in every game. Durant even set a few records. On April 16, 2008, when he was nearly 20 years old, he set career highs for points (42) and rebounds (13). No NBA player had ever scored so many points in a game at such a young age.

Durant also bought a nice house in Seattle and lived there with his mother, who made sure he took care of himself. He loved to play video games, and neighborhood kids would come over to play with him. Sometimes, they even brought cookies.

For his rookie season, Durant averaged 20.3 points, 4.3 rebounds and 2.4 assists. He was just the third teenager to average more than 20 points a game in NBA history. He won rookie of the year. Seattle won only 20 games, but the team was building for the future.

The next year the Supersonics moved to Oklahoma City and changed their name to the Thunder. The move was good for Durant, who improved his averages to 25.3 points, 6.5 rebounds, and 2.8 assists. He set a career high of 47 points against New Orleans.

That set the stage for a huge third season. He became the youngest player (21 years, 197 days) ever to lead the NBA in scoring, with a 30.1-point average. He had three straight 40-point games near the end of the season to edge superstar LeBron James for the scoring title. He also scored at least 25 points in 29 straight games, the second-longest such streak ever in the NBA. He made 756 free throws, the most since Michael Jordan made 833 in the 1986–87 season. He shot 90 percent from the free-throw line, the sixth-best average in league history. Durant was second to James in MVP voting. He also became the second-youngest player (behind James) to score 4,000 career points. Even better, Oklahoma City won 50 games and pushed the Los Angeles Lakers to the limit in a first-round playoff series before losing in six games.

Thunder officials were so impressed, they signed Durant to a five-year contract extension worth $85 million.

Durant was ready to roll for the 2010–11 season. He led Oklahoma City to 55 victories and then to the Western Conference finals. The Thunder lost to the Dallas Mavericks, who went on to beat the Miami Heat, and James, for the NBA championship.

Along the way, Durant made first-team All-NBA and again led the league in scoring (27.7 points). He also averaged 6.8 rebounds and 2.7 assists, and started for the All-Star Team.

Then came the NBA lockout—and five months of uncertainty. Finally, players and owners reached an agreement, with games starting in December of 2011. The season was cut from 82 to 66 games. To make it work, players would have to play a lot of games without much rest. Not every player was ready for that.

Because of his hard workouts, Durant was ready. He led Oklahoma City to 47 wins, the third-most in the league behind Chicago and San Antonio (each won 50). He won his third straight scoring title, this time averaging 28.0 points. That included scoring a team-record of 51 points on February 19, 2012, against Denver.

Next were the playoffs. Durant got better every round. In a four-game, first-round series sweep of Dallas, the defending NBA champion team, Durant averaged 26.5 points and 7.5 rebounds. In five games against the L.A. Lakers and superstar Kobe Bryant in the second round, he averaged 26.8 points and 8.6 rebounds. In the Western Conference finals against favored San Antonio, the no. 1 seeded team, Durant averaged 29.5 points and 6.6 rebounds as the Thunder won the final four games after losing the first two.

That set the stage for a championship battle with the Miami Heat and Durant's good friend, LeBron James.

Durant was too much in the 2012 NBA playoffs, even for Lakers superstar Kobe Bryant.

Durant was ready to show friend and rival LeBron James who had the better team in the 2012 NBA championship series.

Championship Lost, Gold Medal Won

Durant cried. He couldn't help himself. Losing hurts any time, but especially when you're so close to winning a championship.

"I wanted to win as bad as anything in the world," he said. "I cried about it every day."

That lasted about a week, slightly less time than it took for Oklahoma City to lose the best-of-seven NBA championship series in five games to Miami.

The series started great for the Thunder when they won the first game. Then LeBron James and teammates Dwyane Wade and Chris Bosh took charge. The Heat won the next four games to win the championship.

Durant played well, as usual. He averaged 30.6 points and 6 rebounds, but it wasn't enough. In 20 playoff games, he averaged 28.5 points and 7.4 rebounds while rarely resting. Durant averaged a series best of 42 minutes. NBA games last for 48 minutes.

The series ended in late June 2012. Durant didn't have long to feel bad. He and James were both members of the U.S. Olympic basketball team. They got together with the rest of their

teammates—including Kobe Bryant and the Thunder's Russell Westbrook—in July to begin preparing for the Olympics in London. They were together for 39 days under the direction of Duke University's Mike Krzyzewski, the winningest coach in college basketball history.

It was Durant's first Olympics, but not his first international basketball experience. He played on the U.S. team that won the 2010 FIBA World Championships, America's first since 1994.

Durant dominated the world championships by scoring 38 points in a semifinal victory over Lithuania and 28 (including a championship-record seven 3-pointers) in the gold-medal-winning game against Turkey. He also had a 33-point game against Russia. His 22.8-point scoring average broke the U.S. record of 20.2 set by Luther Burden in 1974. Durant was named the tournament's Most Valuable Player.

Durant at the Olympics

Olympic gold was what everyone really wanted. The days when international players were in awe of NBA players were long gone. Now a lot of international players were in the NBA. Everyone knew the Olympics would be tough.

In the 107–100 gold medal win over Spain, Durant scored 30 points. He also scored 28 points against Argentina and 22 against France.

He started all eight Olympic games and led the U.S. in scoring with 19.5 points. Durant's 156 total points set a U.S. Olympic record. He also averaged 5.8 rebounds and 2.6 assists.

Durant's skills were so impressive that NBC commentator and Philadelphia 76er Doug Collins told Thunder basketball writer Nick Gallo, "How quick is his [shooting] release? And how easy does he make those long jump shots look?"

It wasn't easy to beat Spain in the gold medal game. The U.S. led just 90–86 with six minutes left. Then Durant made his fifth three-pointer of the game. Spain never got closer than six points after that.

"It was a very physical game," Krzyzewski told Gallo. "Durant made some huge plays. . . . I thought we had a couple defensive stops and that was [what made the difference]."

What was it like winning a gold medal for the United States?

"You don't just think about the prior two months," Durant told Gallo. "You're thinking about working hard as a 7-, 8-year-old. People telling you that you can't do it. . . . It was just great to finally reach the goal that we had been working toward for a long time. It was like a sigh of relief. . . . Also to do it with that group of guys, so many classy guys and selfless guys, that's what it's all about, playing for your country."

Durant said he worked a lot on his own after practice and by watching his teammates and how they approached workouts and games.

"I think half the game is mental. Just the focus and energy you have to have every single day. The details you have to pay attention to every day. That's why we won the gold.

"For every winning team, it's the small things that win. It's not how many points LeBron scores or Kobe scores or I score. It's the deflections we get, the steals, the blocked shots, the charges we take. Small things separate us because everybody at this level is good at the major things."

Durant said he liked playing with Bryant and James, and that he'd like to play in the 2016 Olympics. "That's my goal, to win another one," he told writer Sean O'Connell. "Hopefully I'm given the chance to do so."

Durant is a versatile guy. Besides playing basketball, he acts and sings, too.

Beyond the Court

There's a lot more to Kevin Durant than what he shows on the court. He's also an actor who played in the 2012 movie *Thunderstruck,* and he hopes to release a rap album some day. He even has a music studio in his house. Durant's a celebrity who sometimes makes the gossip columns. He also earns millions of dollars by helping companies sell their products. For instance, in 2007 he signed a seven-year contract with Nike worth $60 million. In 2012, his Nike shoes cost $140. His Nike retro shirt sold for $120; his T-shirt for $36; and his hat for $26.

Durant also makes $20 million from EA Sports, which produces sports video games, and the soft drink company Gatorade.

How does he spend all this money? Some of the things he splurges on are crab legs and clothing.

Durant isn't afraid of challenges, and that includes acting, although his mother did have to talk him into it. The family comedy *Thunderstruck* began filming during the NBA lockout in 2011, and wrapped in January 2012. Nickelodeon's Taylor Gray, plus veteran actors Brandon T. Jackson and Jim Belushi also starred.

In the movie, Gray plays a Thunder fan who is lousy at basketball until one day he magically gets Durant's skills.

"It's all about conquering your fears," Durant told Associated Press reporter Jeff Latzke. "That's one thing I did with this, stepping in front of a camera and people yelling 'Action!' It's not the norm for me. I did something outside the box, and I'm glad it turned out pretty well.

"A basketball player is what I do. It's not just solely who I am. I like to do other things."

Could acting be Durant's future after he's done with basketball?

Durant got the chance to make a movie because so many fans like him. "When a guy goes over and hugs his mom after the game, that's a guy that people are going to like and that's what you need in a movie," *Thunderstruck* director John Whitesell told Latzke. "You need a guy, a star, who people are going to want to relate to or are going to care about."

People can relate to Durant—and many fans have gotten to know him through Twitter. By early 2013, he had three million followers, in part because he is very honest in his tweets. For instance, he once tweeted, "I do some of the dumbest stuff, just not thinking . . . smh [shaking my head] . . . live and learn though."

Durant is so popular that in the summer of 2012, sports video game company 2K Sports rated him ahead of Kobe Bryant for the first time although he was still behind Michael Jordan and LeBron James.

Durant has several tattoos, but he doesn't like showing them off because it's not good for business (tattoos can turn off some fans and customers). He has them on his back and chest, so no one can see them when he's wearing a basketball uniform. On his back, the word Maryland, stretches from shoulder to shoulder. There's a tattoo of a boy dribbling a basketball while wearing the number 35, which honors his former AAU coach, Charles Craig, who was murdered at the age of 35 while Durant was in middle school. Durant also wears that number for the Thunder.

He sponsors the Kevin Durant Family Foundation, which supports summer programs and afterschool programs, donates to single parents, helps childhood education, and more.

All this is possible because of basketball. Yet, in 2012 Durant told the *Washington Post* he isn't close to reaching his potential: "I've heard a few times, that in three or four years, 'this league is going to be yours.' . . . I don't like that. Because I think I'm established now. My time is now. I feel as though I've proved myself these last five years that I can be one of the top players in the league. I've got a long way to go to being the ultimate best, but I think my time is now. And I'm starting to enter my prime."

That's an interesting thought given how much Durant has already accomplished, but it's exactly what he learned from his mother. Wanda Pratt said she wants Durant, and her two other sons, to be "well rounded," to "always give everything that you have," and to be "a man he could look up to."

Durant has done that. In the end, he's much more than just a kid at heart.

NBA
Career Statistics

Year	Team	GP	GS	MPG	FG%	3P%	FT%	RPG	APG	SPG	BPG	PPG
2007–08	Seattle	80	80	34.6	.430	.288	.873	4.4	2.4	1.0	.9	20.3
2008–09	Oklahoma City	74	74	39.0	.476	.422	.863	6.5	2.8	1.3	.7	25.3
2009–10	Oklahoma City	82	82	39.5	.476	.365	.900	7.6	2.8	1.4	1.0	30.1
2010–11	Oklahoma City	78	78	38.9	.462	.350	.880	6.8	2.7	1.1	1.0	27.7
2011–12	Oklahoma City	66	66	38.6	.496	.387	.860	8.0	3.5	1.3	1.2	28.0
2012–13	Oklahoma City	81	81	38.5	.510	.416	.905	7.9	4.6	1.4	1.3	28.1
Career		461	461	38.2	.475	.373	.884	6.8	3.1	1.3	1.0	26.6
All-Star		4	3	29.8	.523	.367	.875	5.3	1.5	1.8	.5	28.8

Playoffs

Year	Team	GP	GS	MPG	FG%	3P%	FT%	RPG	APG	SPG	BPG	PPG
2010	Oklahoma City	6	6	38.5	.350	.286	.871	7.7	2.3	.5	1.3	25.0
2011	Oklahoma City	17	17	42.5	.449	.339	.838	8.2	2.8	.9	1.1	28.6
2012	Oklahoma City	20	20	41.9	.517	.373	.864	7.4	3.7	1.4	1.2	28.5
2013	Oklahoma City	11	11	44.1	45.5	31.4	83.0	9.0	6.3	1.3	1.1	30.8
Career		43	43	41.6	.465	.346	.854	7.7	3.2	1.1	1.2	28.1

1988   Kevin Wayne Durant is born to Wanda Durant and Wayne Pratt on September 29, in Washington, D.C. His parents divorce. Durant is raised by his mother and grandmother.

2002   He attends Montrose Christian School in Rockville, Maryland.

2004   Durant spends his junior year at Oak Hill Academy in Virginia.

2006   He graduates from Montrose National Christian Academy, and is recruited by the University of Texas.

2007   Durant is named ESPN All-American and AP All-America, and receives multiple national college Player of the Year awards. He leaves Texas to join the NBA, where the Seattle SuperSonics draft him as the no. 2 pick.

2008   Durant averages 20.3 points per game and is named NBA Rookie of the Year. The Seattle SuperSonics are sold to Oklahoma City and change their name to the Thunder.

2009   Durant averages 25.3 points per game and is the All-Star H-O-R-S-E competition winner.

2010   He competes internationally at the FIBA World Championship, earning the MVP award; he is an NBA All-Star; and he is the youngest player to be named NBA scoring champion (with an average of 30.1 points per game, and scoring 30 or more points in 7 straight games). Durant is again the NBA All-Star H-O-R-S-E competition winner and is named to the All-NBA first team. He signs a five-year contract extension with the Thunder, worth $85 million.

2011   Again, Durant is an NBA All-Star and the NBA scoring champ (27.7 points per game). During the NBA lockout, he continues to practice and work out hard. The lockout ends in December.

2012   The Kevin Durant Family Foundation is formed. Durant is the NBA scoring champ (28.0 points per game) and MVP of the NBA All-Star Game, in which he scores 36 points. He plays on the gold-medal Olympic team with superstars LeBron James and Kobe Bryant.

2013   Durant's streak of three straight NBA scoring titles ends when he finishes second to New York's Carmelo Anthony. Durant averages 28.1 points to Anthony's 28.7.

Books

Doeden, Matt. *Kevin Durant, Basketball Superstar.* New York: Sports Illustrated Kids, 2012.

Gitlin, Marty. *Kevin Durant: NBA Superstar.* Minneapolis: Sportszone, 2012.

Sandler, Michael. *Kevin Durant.* New York: Bearport Publishing, 2012.

Savage, Jeff. *Kevin Durant.* Minneapolis: Lerner Publishing Co., 2012.

Works Consulted

Gallo, Nick. "Durant Improved from Team USA Experience." http://www.nba.com/thunder/olympics_durant_120822.html

Gallo, Nick. "Team USA Takes Home the Gold." NBA.com, n.d. http://www.nba.com/thunder/olympics_120812.html

"Kevin Durant's Mother, Wanda Pratt." http://www.playerwives.com/nba/ oklahoma-city-thunder/kevin-durants-mother-wanda-pratt/

Lee, Michael. "Kevin Durant: 'My time is now.' " *Washington Post,* August 25, 2012. http://www.washingtonpost.com/sports/wizards/kevin-durant-my-time-is-now/2012/08/25/781f0628-ee3b-11e1-afd6-f55f84bc0c41_story. html

St. Weir, Tom. "Kevin Durant jumps into flag football game at Okla." *USA Today,* November 1, 2011. http://content.usatoday.com/ communities/gameon/post/2011/11/kevin-durant-jumps-into-flag-football-game-at-okla-st/1#.UEF1BaCCkoM

Smith, Michael. "Durant Gets Thunderstruck." *Tulsa World,* August 22, 2012. http://www.tulsaworld.com/blogs/post.aspx?Kevin_Durant_gets_ Thunderstruck/5-16611

Thomsen, Ian. "The New Era—Heat vs. Thunder." *Sports Illustrated,* June 18, 2012.

Yorkey, Mike, with Joshua Cooley and Jesse Florea. *Playing With Purpose.* Uhrichsville, Ohio: Barbour Publishing, 2012.

On the Internet

Kevin Durant Biography
    http://www.jockbio.com/Bios/Durant/Durant_bio.html

Kevin Durant Official Web Site
    http://kevindurant35.com/

NBA.com Kevin Durant Player Profile
    http://www.nba.com/playerfile/kevin_durant/

Amateur Athletic Union (AAU)—A United States organization dedicated to the promotion and development of amateur athletes.

defensive back—A player who covers the other team's receivers to try to stop them from catching passes in football.

flag football—A non-contact football game in which players are "tackled" by pulling flags off their waists.

forward—An inside position on a basketball team.

fraternity—A social organization of male college students.

free throw—A basketball shot taken from a designated line while play is stopped.

fundraiser—An event that helps raise money for a charity or worthy cause.

gold medal—The trophy for taking first place in an Olympic event.

MVP—Most Valuable Player. An award given to a league's best player as determined by a vote.

NBA—National Basketball Association. The governing body of professional basketball in the United States.

NBA lockout—A total stop in league activity, usually while new contracts are being debated.

Olympics—A major international sports competition held every four years.

playoffs—A set of games played between the top teams in a league to determine who will play in the championship game.

potential—Possible, but not yet realized; an ability that still needs to be developed.

quarterback—In football games, the leader of the offense who can pass, run, or hand off the football.

rebound—To grab a missed shot.

recruit—To find an outstanding player and convince him or her to play for a particular team.

rookie—A newcomer or first-year player in a league.

three-pointer—A long-distance shot; in the NBA, a shot taken from beyond the arc (line) that is about 23.75 feet from the basket.

tweet—A short message sent through the social access site Twitter.